Mary Jane

M000097081

Welcome!

Radiant Earth is a compilation of patterns and ideas that derive from my own enjoyment and admiration of God's creation. I hope that you will enjoy these designs and in between stitching, take time to awaken to the beauty around you.

Best wishes and happy stitching!

☆☆☆☆☆☆☆☆☆☆☆☆☆☆☆☆☆☆☆☆☆☆☆☆☆☆

Acknowledgements

This book would not have been possible without the help of many friends and the loving patience of my family, John, Zac, Eli, Josh, and Hannah. Thanks to each of these very special people.

Business Manager	Gloria Pandolph
Appliqué Samples	Barbara Bradley
	Claudia Atchison
	Donna Buchorn
	Alvasyne Pace
Hand Quilting	Cathy Nihiser
Rug Hooking	Barbara Bentley
Photography	Jimmy Prybil
Cover design	John Gilmore
Formatting	Pat and Catherine Springle
Encourager	Pat Rabon

Table of Contents

☆☆☆☆☆☆☆☆☆☆☆☆☆☆☆☆☆☆☆☆☆☆☆☆☆☆

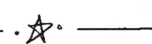 

General Instructions

This book has been published for the express purpose of sharing the designs for quilting, needlework, and rug hooking. This is not a how-to book. I encourage you to visit your local quilt shop and participate in the classes given by qualified teachers. Quilt guilds are also a great resource for everyone that would like to know more about the art of quilting.

All seams are 1/4" and are included in the piecing measurements.

Fabric: Use 100 % cotton fabric whenever possible, especially for appliqué.
Cotton holds a crease well while appliquéing and it doesn't fray easily when stitching points. Cotton has stood the test of time and will endure through the years. This is an important point if you value your hand work. Fabric used in these designs were 45" in width.

Thread: Use 100 % cotton thread for piecing. Use a fine, machine embroidery or silk thread for appliqué, matching the thread color with the appliqué design, not the background. For the needlework, 2 strands of embroidery thread were used unless noted otherwise.

Batting: I use a cotton batt that is as thin as possible so that the finished quilt looks old.

Appliqué Designs: The appliqué designs in this book were designed for needle turn appliqué. If you fuse these designs they must be reversed if they are directional.

Appliqué: Trace appliqué design onto unwaxed side of freezer paper. Cut the design pieces out of freezer paper on the lines. Press waxed side of paper down onto the right side of selected fabric. Using a brown or black fine point pen, trace around each design. Cut designs out leaving 1/8" - 1/4" of fabric from line. Glue or baste design in place. Turn designs under with needle, including the line, and stitch.

Needlework: All needle work is stitched on 2 layers of pre-washed muslin. This provides enough thickness so that threads can not be seen through your work. Using a light box, trace design onto top layer of muslin with a pencil.

Tea-dye: When the needlework is complete, soak with water. I use a spray bottle and wet the work through. In another spray bottle I mix a strong brew of instant tea. Spray onto needlework until you have achieved the desired effect. You can always spray more water on the fabric to lighten the tea. Dry in the sun or on top of your clothes dryer.

Liberty Thistle

Size: 57"x 59" Wall Quilt
25" x 27" Hooked Rug

This design was used for a hooked rug which depicts one of the squares in the quilt. Kits are available through Cabin Fever Designs. All wool is hand dyed and pre-cut with design drawn on burlap.

Fabric Requirements:
Background blocks,
Outer Zigzag border,
& Inner sashing & border ......3 yds
Inner Zigzag,
& Outer border......2 yds

Appliqué Design:
Hearts......1/2 yd
1st Thistle & Triangles in border......1 yd
2nd Thistle......1/2 yd
Leaves......3/4 yd
Stems......1/2 yd

Instructions:
☆ Cut 4 background blocks - 21 1/2" x 23".
☆ Cut out 4 each of Thistle 1a, 1b and 1c.
☆ Cut out 4 each of Thistle 2a and 2b, and 4 reverse designs of Thistle 2a and 2b.
☆ Cut out 4 each of Leaves 1, 2, and 3 and 4 reverse designs of each leaf.
☆ Cut out 4 center stems and 4 each of stem 1 and 4 reverse designs of stem 1.
☆ Cut out 8 Hearts, 1 for each of the 4 blocks and 4 for the border corners.
☆ Cut out 24 triangles for border design.
☆ Cut out 16 - 23" inner zigzag designs for trim on blocks.
☆ Cut out 4 outer zigzag designs. The length of

these will be determined by your finished quilt size. Start out with pieces the width of the fabric (45") and trim the length down appropriately.
☆ Cut 4 - 1 1/4" strips for sashing and inner border.
☆ Cut 6 - 6 1/2" strips for outer border.
☆ Appliqué Thistle and Heart design on each of the 4 blocks. Be sure to center your design and allow for seam allowances.
☆ Cut inner zigzag design out and appliqué to the raw edges of each block. Stitch only the inner zigzag edge. The outer edge should be even with the raw edge of the block and will be caught in the seam allowance when completed.
☆ Sew the 4 blocks together with the 1 1/4" sashing. (Finished sashing width is 3/4".)

☆ Sew remaining 1 1/4" strips to outer edge of quilt blocks.

☆ Cut out and appliqué the outer zigzag design to the outer border strips. The zig-zag design should end evenly with the inner border corners.

☆ Appliqué the 4 border Hearts to both ends of the side borders with points directed into the quilt from all 4 corners.

☆ Sew the top and bottom borders to the quilt.

☆ Sew the side borders onto the quilt.

☆ Stitch veins in leaves with black embroidery thread and long running stitch.

☆ Quilting is a 1" cross-hatch design inside the blocks. The border is quilted in stripes where not appliquéd.

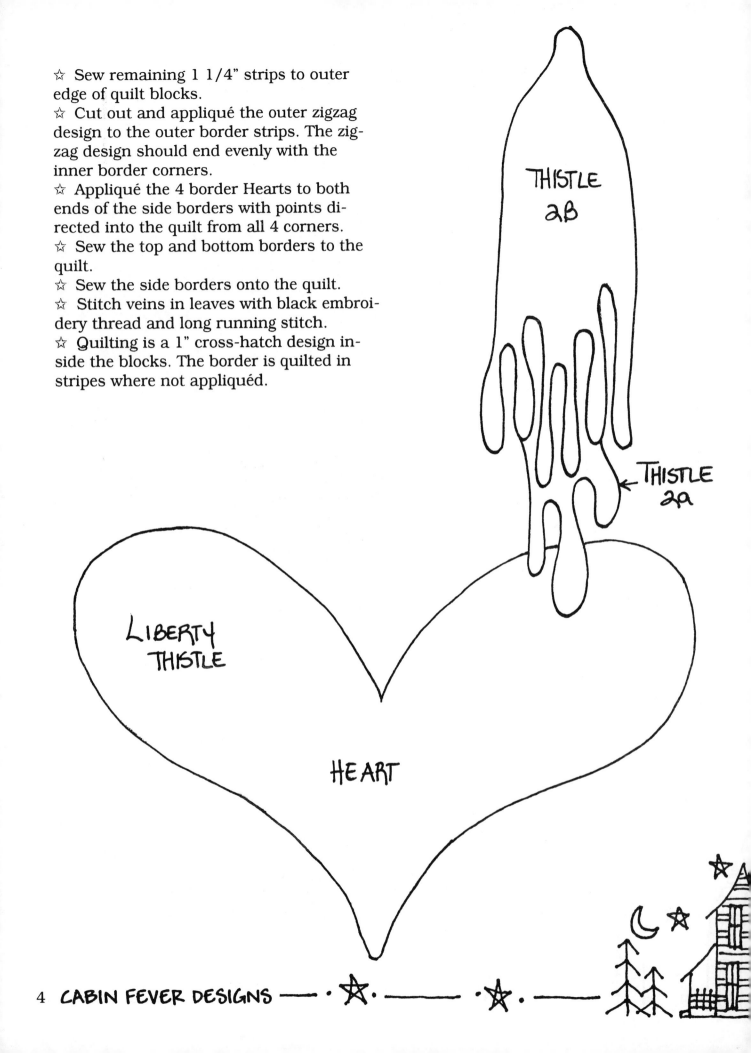

THISTLE 2B

← THISTLE 2a

LIBERTY THISTLE

HEART

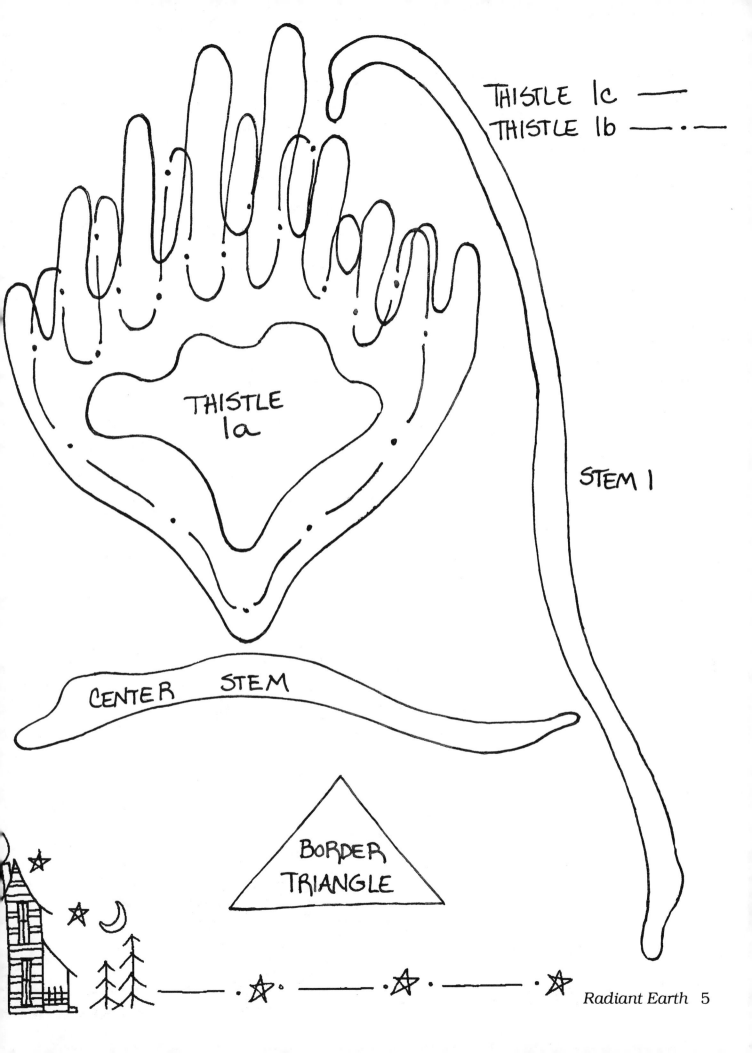

THISTLE 1c ———
THISTLE 1b —·—

THISTLE 1a

STEM 1

CENTER STEM

BORDER TRIANGLE

Radiant Earth 5

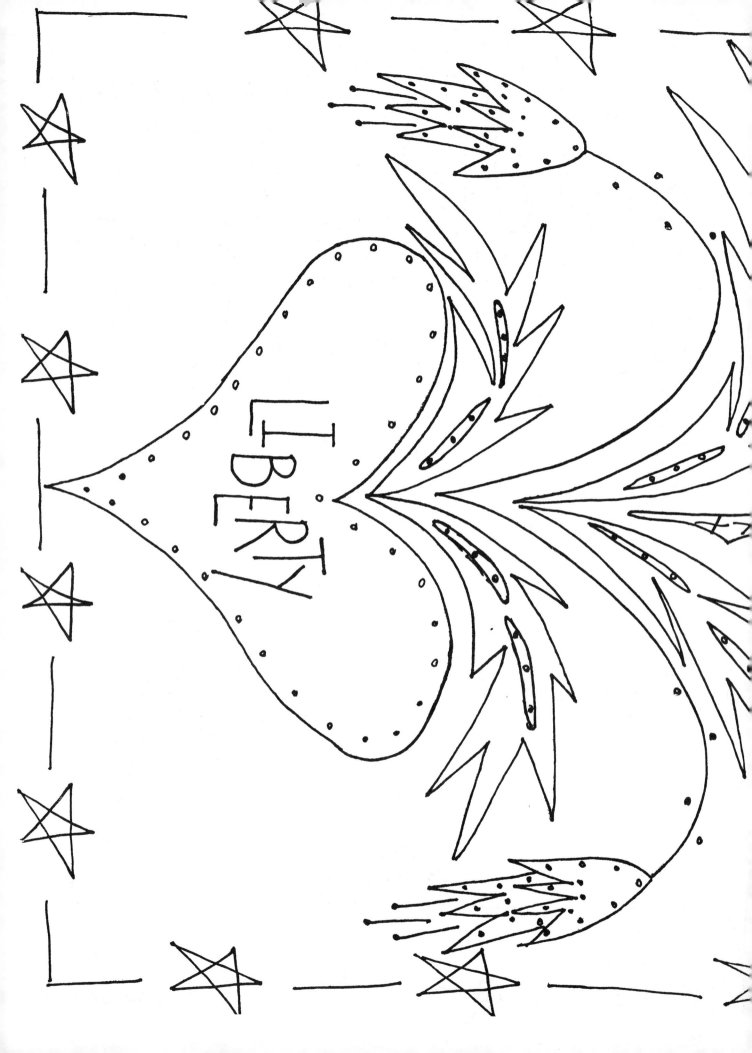

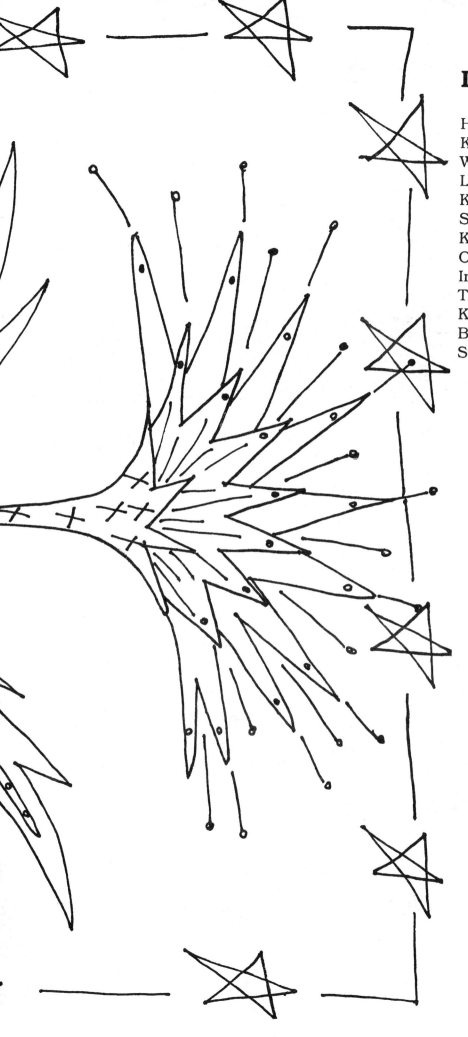

Liberty Thistle

Heart/ Red....816
Knots on Heart/ Red....816
Words/ Black....310
Leaves/ Green....3012
Knots on Leaves/ Green....936
Stems/ Green....936
Knots on Stem/ Green....936
Outer Thistle/ Purple....315
Inner Thistle/ Purple....3726
Thistle Centers/ Lt. Green....734
Knots on Thistles/ Purple....315
Border Lines/ Black....310
Stars/ Gold....680

Morning Glory

Size: 24" x 48" Wall Quilt

This quilt was designed for placement above the mantle.

Size: 24" x 48" Hooked Rug

This design was used for a hooked rug. Kits are available through Cabin Fever Designs. All wool is hand dyed and pre-cut with design drawn on burlap.

Fabric Requirements:

Background...... 1/2 yd
Border......1/2 yd
Zigzag border and Flowers......1/2 yd
Lg. Circles and Halos......1/4 yd
Stars and Halos......1/4 yd
Sm. Circles......1/8 yd
Heart......6" x 9"
Wings......8" x 8"
Dresses......12" x 12"
Heads, Hands, and Feet......6" x 6"
Leaves and Stems......12" x 15"

Instructions:

☆ Cut 1 - 16" x 40" rectangle for background.
☆ Cut 3 - 4" strips for the border. 2 side borders - 16" long
and 1 top and bottom border - 48" each.
☆ Cut 1 heart. Cut 1 small star. Cut 1 each of the angel and flowers design and 1 each of the reverse angel and flowers design.
☆ Cut 12 Lg. circles and 12 Lg. stars. Cut 30 Sm. circles.
☆ Cut out zigzag design for border; 2 lengths with 2 points, 1 length with 3 points, 1 length with 4 points, 2 lengths with 5 points, 1 length with 7 points.
☆ Appliqué angels and flowers design on the background block.
☆ Appliqué heart and star centering it

under the flowers.
☆ Appliqué borders. Zigzag design is appliquéd so that the straight raw edge is placed along the inside border and points are directed outward; Top border starting with the left corner - Lg. circle with star, 1 - 5 point zigzag, 3 Lg. circles with Lg. stars, 1 - 5 point zigzag, 1 Lg. circle with Lg. star. Appliqué Sm. circles in between each point on zigzag for a total of 8.
☆ Bottom border starting at left corner - Lg. circle with Lg. star, 1 - 4 point zigzag, 1 Lg. circle with Lg. star, 1 - 7 point zigzag, 2 Lg. circles with Lg. stars. Appliqué Sm. circles in between each point on zigzag for a total of 9.
☆ Left border starting at the top - 1 - 3 point zigzag, 2 Lg. circles with 2 Lg. stars. Appliqué Sm. circles in between each point on zigzag for a total of 2.
☆ Right border starting at the top - 1 - 2 point zigzag, 1 Lg. circle with Lg. star, 1 - 2 point zigzag. Appliqué Sm. circles in between each point on the zigzag for a total of 2.
☆ Stitch eyes on angels with black embroidery thread.
☆ Quilting is done in a diagonal on the background 1 1/2" apart. Remaining quilting is done around appliqué designs.

—·— —·— ·— ·—

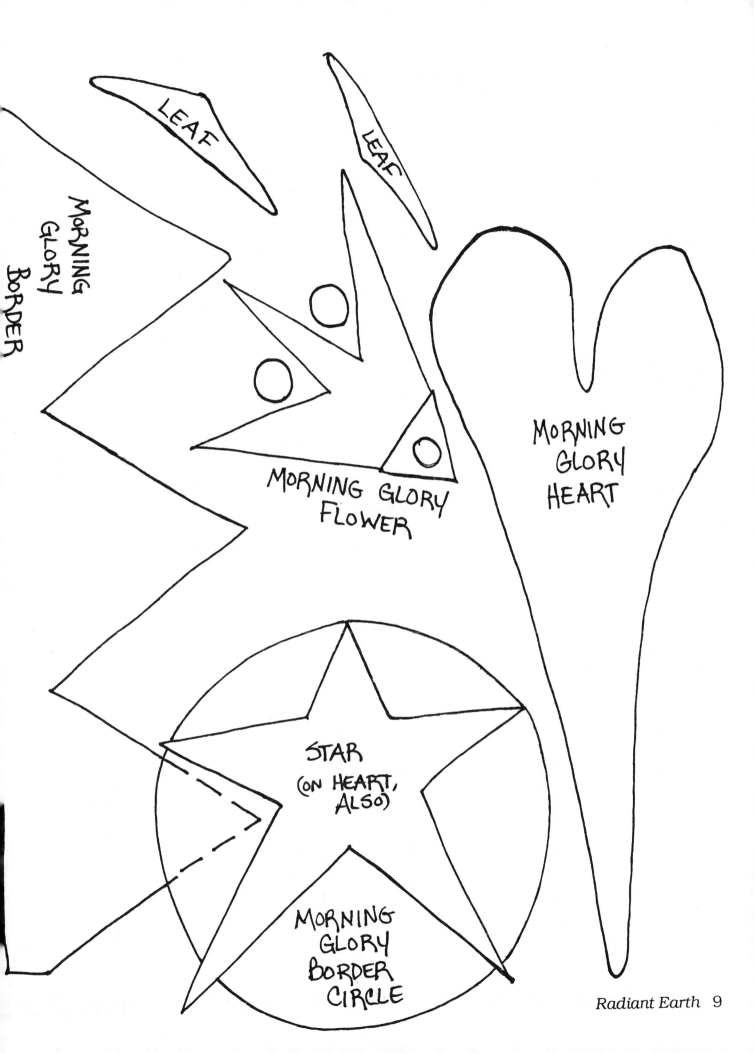

LEAF

LEAF

MORNING GLORY BORDER

MORNING GLORY FLOWER

MORNING GLORY HEART

STAR
(ON HEART, ALSO)

MORNING GLORY BORDER CIRCLE

Radiant Earth

Size: 27 3/4" x 30 3/4"

Fabric Requirements:
Background Center Square
& Flying Geese Rectangles......1 yd
Flying Geese Squares &
Corner triangles......1/3 yd
Inner Border & Corners......1/4 yd
Outer Border......1/4 yd

Appliqué Designs:
Stems & Leaf veins......1/2 yd
Circle Flowers......1 fat quarter
Centers & Stripes......12" square
Hearts......8" square
Leaves & Upper stems......1 fat quarter
Circles under stripes on flowers......8"
square
Radiant earth in center......12" square
Lg center circle......6" square
Sm center circle......3" square

Instructions:
☆ Cut 1 background center square - 20" x
20".
☆ For Flying Geese, cut 12 - 3 1/2" x
6 1/2" rectangles and 16 - 3 1/2" x 3 1/2"
squares.
☆ Cut 4 - 6 7/8" squares for corner triangles.
☆ Cut 2 - 1 1/2" strips for the inner border.
☆ Cut 4 - 1 7/8" x 3 1/4" rectangles for
the corners of the inner border. (small
flying geese)
☆ Cut 3 - 2" strips for the outer border.
☆ Cut 8 - 1 7/8" squares for the corners
of the inner border. (small flying geese)
These squares are the same fabric as the
outer border. This will make sense when
the piecing is done.

For the Appliqué:
☆ Cut 1 large center stem and 4 corner
stems.
☆ Cut 4 large circle flowers and 12 small
circle flowers.
☆ Cut 4 flower stripes and 4 stripe circle
strips. These strips will fit under the
stripes and will be reverse appliquéd.
☆ Cut 12 flower centers.
☆ Cut 4 Hearts.
☆ Cut 2 large leaves and 2 vein strips.
☆ Cut 2 medium leaves and 2 vein
strips.
☆ Cut 8 small leaves and 8 vein strips.
☆ Cut 12 upper stems
☆ Appliqué center design onto back-
ground square. Reverse
appliqué flower stripe circles
and leaf veins.
☆ Sew 1 1/2"

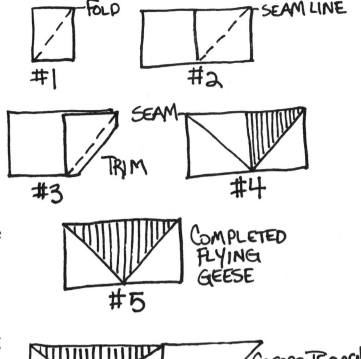

inner border strips to the top, bottom and sides of the center block. Set aside.

☆ Assemble 8 flying geese in the following manner. (Numbers correspond to designs shown on these pages.)

1. Fold the flying geese squares in half diagonally.

2. Sew, along the fold line, the square to one end of each of 8 flying geese rectangles.

3. Trim 1/4" from seam. Press.

4. Sew a flying geese square to the opposite end of each of the above 8 flying geese rectangles.

5. Trim 1/4" from seam. Press. At this point you should have 8 complete flying geese rectangles and 4 remaining flying geese rectangles. Set the 4 remaining flying geese rectangles aside and work only with the 8 complete flying geese.

6. Sew the above complete flying geese into sets of 2. Press. You will have 4 sets of 2.

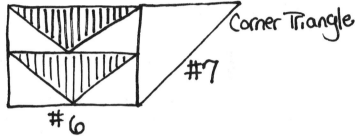

7. Take the 4 - 6 7/8" squares and cut them in half diagonally. Sew a triangle to one side of each of the 4 sets of 2. Press.

8. Sew the remaining triangles to the other side of each of the 4 sets of 2. Press.

9. Sew the remaining flying geese rectangles, that were set aside, to the end of each of the above sets. Press. Trim this rectangle so that the entire piece is a triangle.

10. Center and sew a triangle section to each side of the center block. Press. Set aside.

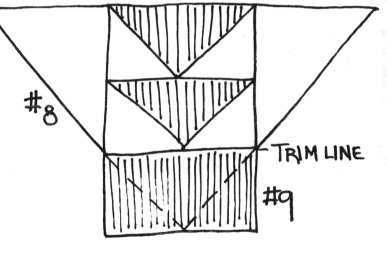

11. Assemble the small flying geese for the inner border corners in the same manner you assembled the larger flying geese. You will have 4 small flying geese. The flying geese will be the corners of the inner border. They must be centered on the sides of the quilt. Cut the outer border strips into 8 - 15" x 2" strips. Sew one strip to either end of the small flying geese.

12. Sew an outer border strip to the top, bottom, and sides of the quilt. Center the points. Press.

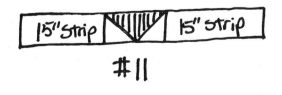

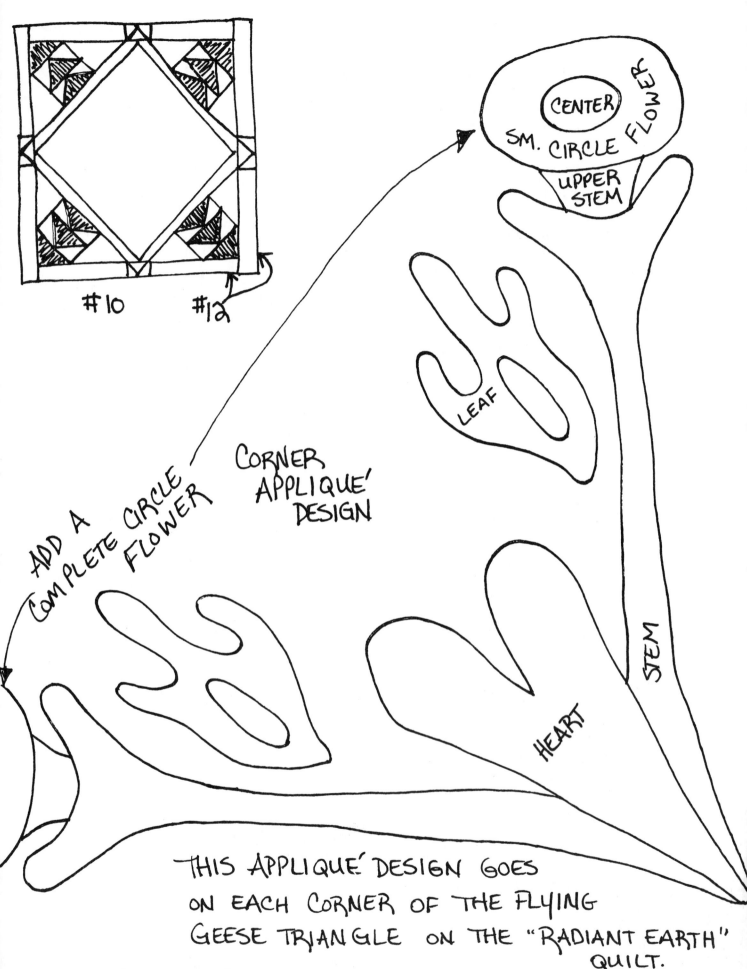

#10   #12

CENTER

SM. CIRCLE FLOWER

UPPER STEM

LEAF

HEART

STEM

ADD A COMPLETE CIRCLE FLOWER

CORNER APPLIQUÉ DESIGN

THIS APPLIQUÉ DESIGN GOES ON EACH CORNER OF THE FLYING GEESE TRIANGLE ON THE "RADIANT EARTH" QUILT.

Garden Pocket Pouch (Purse)

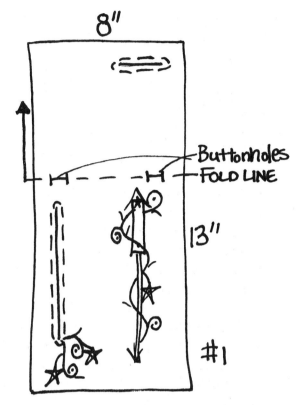

Fabric Requirements:

1/3 yd osnaberg muslin (tea-dyed)
1/4 yd lining fabric
embroidery thread:
310 - black
680 - gold
3051 - green

Instructions:

☆ Cut 1 - 8" x 13" rectangle (purse back) from muslin and 1 from lining fabric.
☆ Cut 1 - 8" x 20 1/2" (purse front w/flap) rectangle from muslin and 1 from lining fabric.
☆ Cut 1 - 4 1/2" square (tab) from muslin.
☆ Cut 1 - 2" x desired length (purse strap) from muslin.
☆ Transfer needle work design to purse front and flap on right side of muslin.

Remember: The flap will be folding over the top of the purse back so the design must go in the appropriate direction. When stitched, it will be upside down when looking at the purse front w/flap. (Diagram 1)
—After completing the needlework, mark slits on the wrong side of the muslin. With right sides together, sew a 1/4" seam around the slit lines on the muslin and lining. The openings are only on the purse front w/flap. Dimensions are as follows:
—The purse front opening is 6" from the bottom and 1 1/2" from the left front. The slit line is 6" long. (Diagram 2)
—The flap opening is 1" from bottom of flap (when folded over) and 1" from left flap back. The slit line is 2" long. (Diagram 3)
—After sewing 1/4" around the slit lines, cut fabric on lines through both muslin and lining. Turn right side

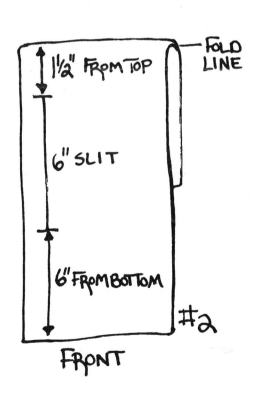

out and press. Stitch running stitch with black embroidery thread 1/4" around opening.

—Sew tab and purse strap each with 1/4" seam along long edge, right sides together. Turn right side out and press. Turn under raw edges and finish. Make a buttonhole at one end of the tab and sew the opposite end onto the purse back 5 1/2" from bottom edge and 1 1/4" from left side. (Diagram 4)

—Turn under 1/4" on the bottom edge of the flap and the top edge of the purse back and finish seam. Place purse front w/flap right side up on work surface. Place the purse back down on top of purse front right sides together, matching bottom edges. Sew 1/4" seam from top of purse back down the side, across the bottom, and up the other side. ——Clip corners and turn right side out. Press.

—Sew buttonholes on the fold line at both sides of the flap for the strap to go through. Thread the ends of strap through the buttonhole on the flap and stitch ends of strap onto the inside of the purse.

—Thread the tab through the slit on the flap and mark placement of button on purse back. You are now ready to take off to the antique fields or the quilt show with a handy pouch for carrying your necessities. Enjoy!

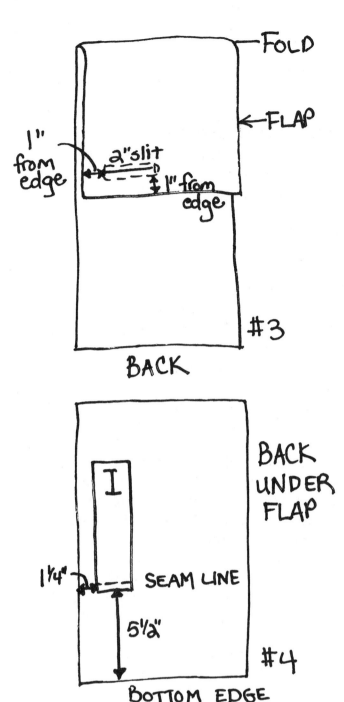

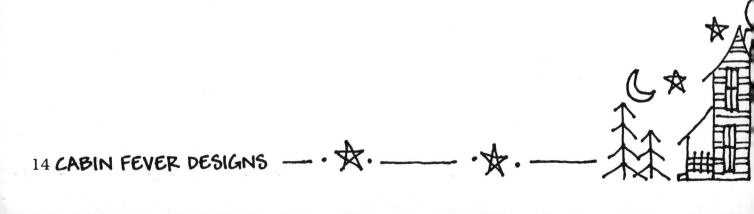

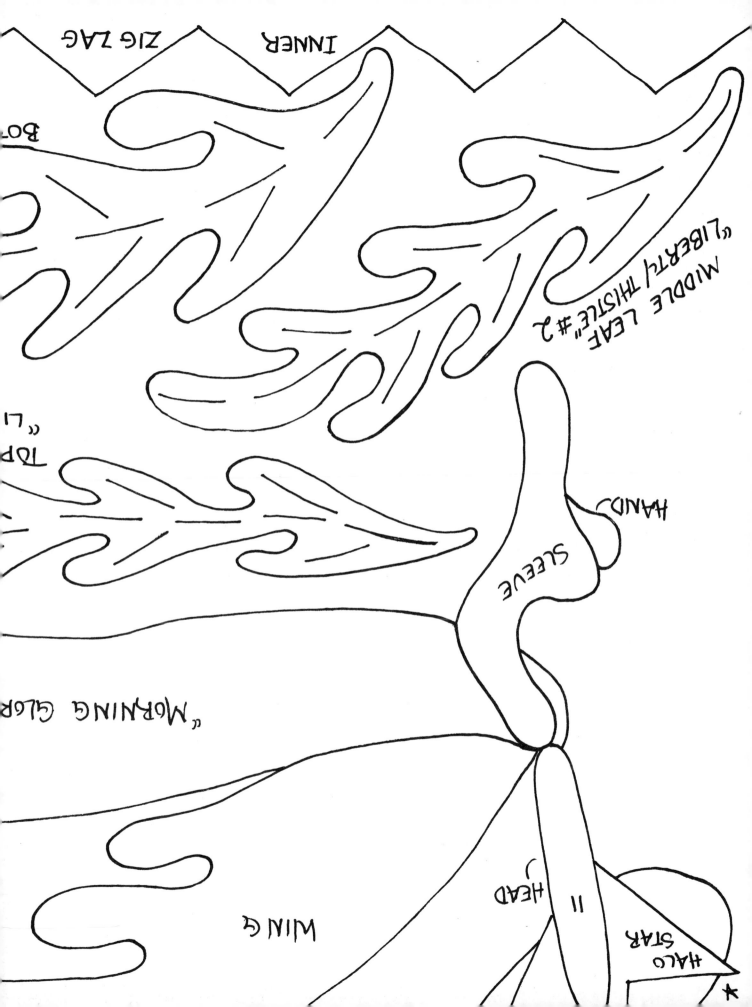

ZIG ZAG   INNER

BOT

"LIBERTY THISTLE"#2
MIDDLE LEAF

"LI
TOP

HANDS
SLEEVE

"MORNING GLOR

WING   HEAD   II

HALO
STAR

*

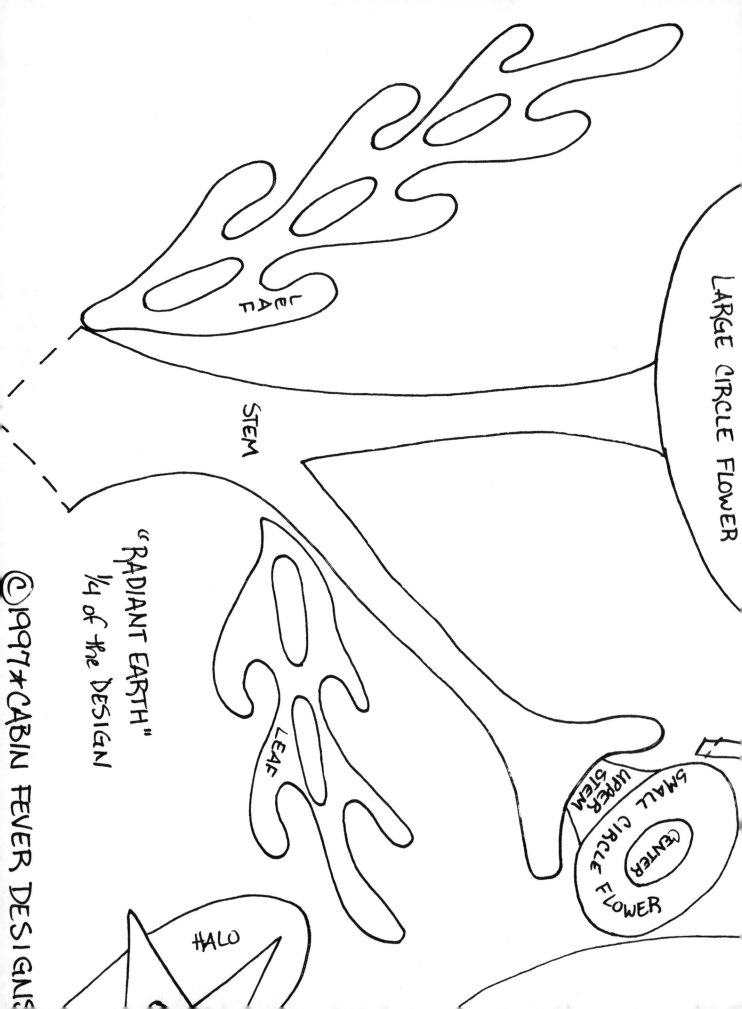

LARGE CIRCLE FLOWER

LEAF

STEM

"RADIANT EARTH"
¼ of the DESIGN

LEAF

SMALL CIRCLE
FLOWER
CENTER
UPPER STEM

HALO

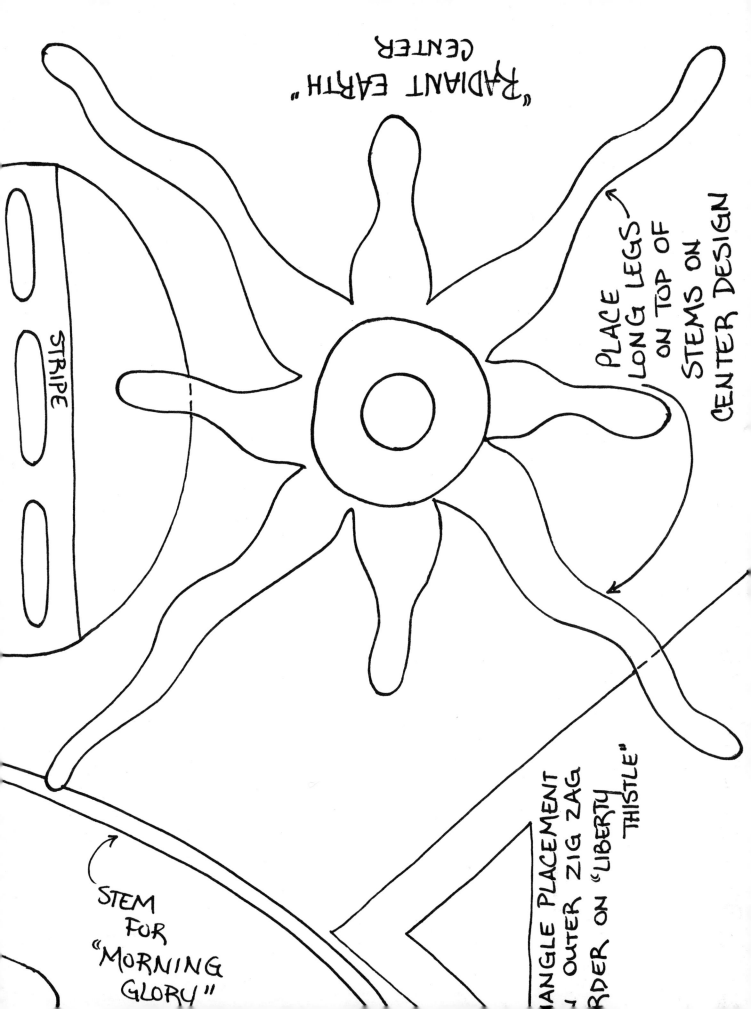

"RADIANT EARTH"
CENTER

PLACE LONG LEGS ON TOP OF STEMS ON CENTER DESIGN

STRIPE

STEM FOR "MORNING GLORY"

ANGLE PLACEMENT 1 OUTER ZIG ZAG RDER ON "LIBERTY THISTLE"

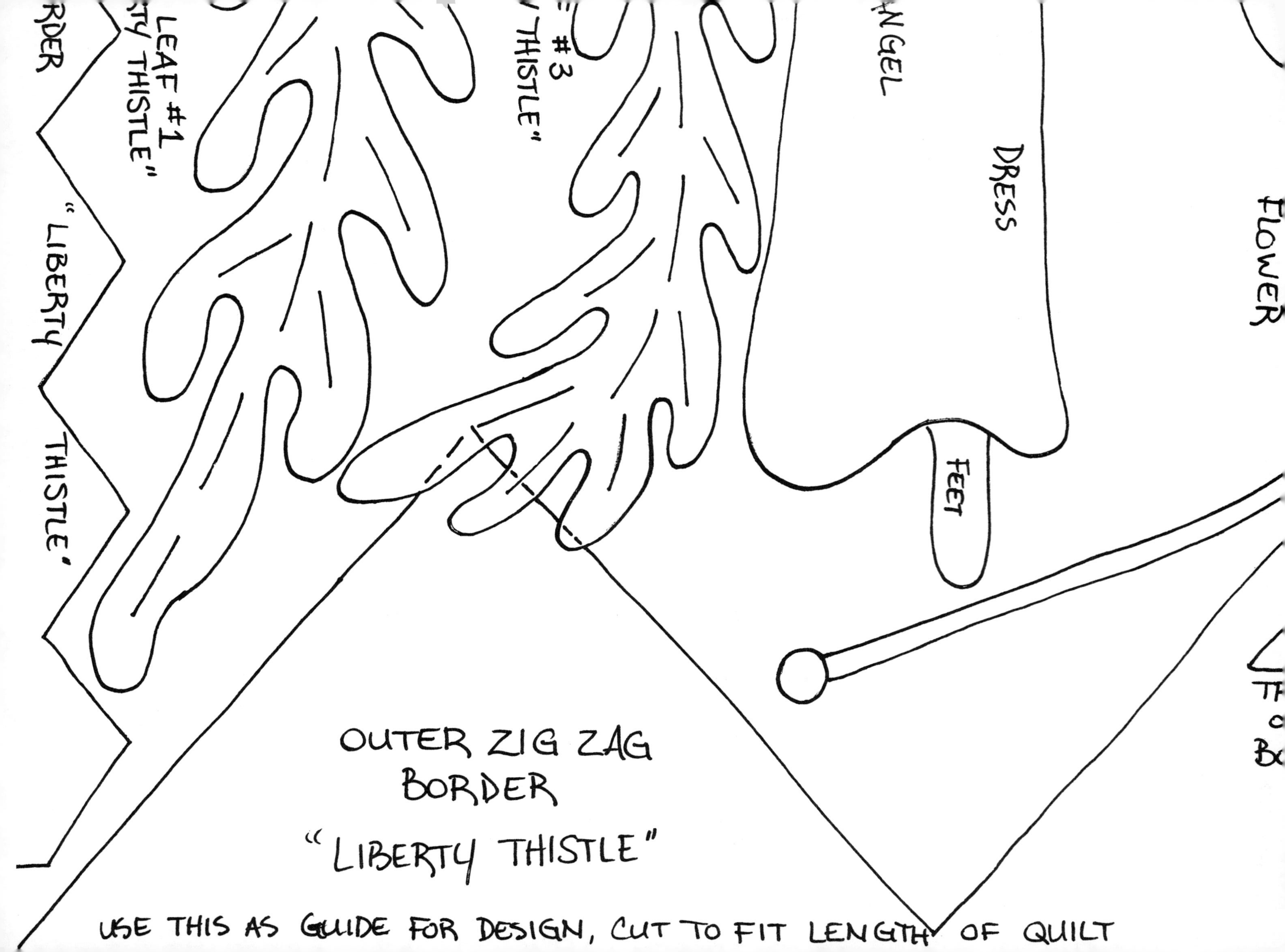

USE THIS AS GUIDE FOR DESIGN, CUT TO FIT LENGTH OF QUILT

OUTER ZIG ZAG
BORDER
"LIBERTY THISTLE"

"LIBERTY THISTLE"

"LIBERTY THISTLE"

LEAF #1

#3

THISTLE"

ANGEL

DRESS

FEET

FLOWER

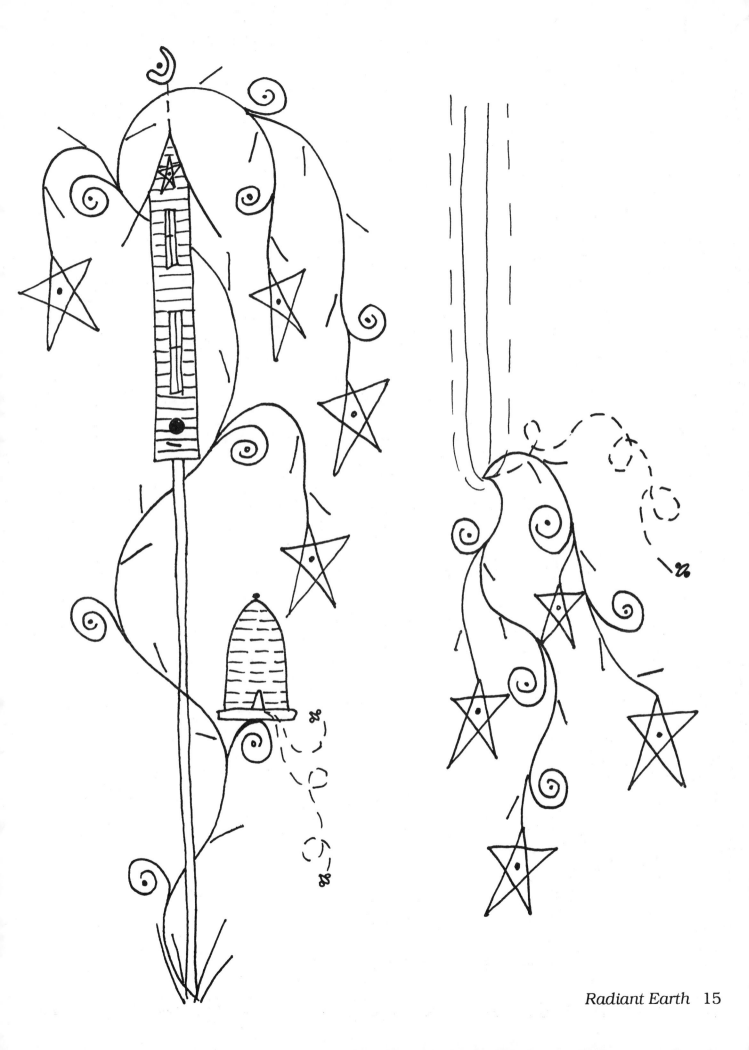

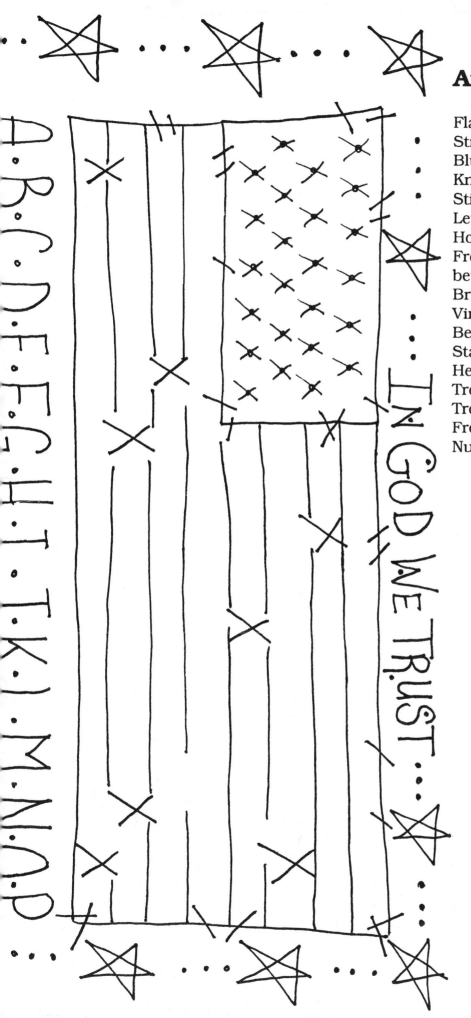

Americana Sampler

Flags:
Stripes/ Red....816
Blue Field/ Blue....930
Knots & X's on Blue Field/ Ecru
Stitches on Flag/ Black....310
Letters & Numbers/ Black....310
House & Windows/ Black....310
French knots on Border &
between Stars/ Black....310
Bricks/ Red....816
Vines/ Green....936
Berries/ Blue....930
Stars & Moon/ Gold....680
Hearts/ Red....816
Tree Trunks/ Brown....3031
Tree Branches/ Green....936
French knots between Letters &
Numbers/ Gold....680

© 1997 Cabin Fever

Large Heart
with Birdhouses

Heart/ Red....816
French knots on Heart/ Red....816
Birdhouses, Windows,
Roof, Poles/Black....310
Boards on Birdhouses/ Brown....3031
Vines/ Green....936
Stars & Moon/ Lt. Gold....676
Lazy Daisies/ Gold....680
Centers/ Brown....3031
Flowers/Ecru
Centers/Lt. Gold....676
Border Lines/ Black....310

4 Minis

Mini USA

Flag Stripes/ Red....816
Heart/ Red....816
French knots on Heart/ Red....816
Blue Field/ Blue....930
Writing/ Blue....930
French knots on blue field/ Ecru
Stitches on Flag/ Black....310
Border/ Black....310
Border Stars/ Gold....680

Mini Heart

Heart/ Red....816
 French knots on Heart/ Red....816
  Lines on Heart/ Black.....310
   Writing/ Black....310
    Vine/ Green....936
     Flowers/ Blue....794
      Centers/ Lt. Gold....676
       French knots/ Gold....680
        Border/ Black....310

Mini Birdhouse

Birdhouse/ Brown....3031
Birdhouse Boards/ Ecru
Birdhouse Windows & Hole/ Black....310
Birdhouse Base/ Black....310
French knots on Base/ Brown....3031
Bird/ Black....310
Moon & Stars/ Gold....680
Flowers/ Purple....3726
Centers/ Gold....680
Stems/ Green....3012
French knots on Stems/ Green....936
Leaves/ Green....3012
Grass/ Green....936
French knots on grass/ Green....3012
Border Lines/ Green....936
Border French knots/ Ecru

Mini Bee Skep

Bee Skep/ Lt. Gold....676
Heart/ Red....816
Vine, Stems, Leaves/ Green....936
Lazy Daisies/ Ecru
Centers/ Orange....976
Flowers/ Pink....758
Centers/ Ecru
Bee/ Black....310
French knots on Bee/ Gold....680
Border/ Black....310
French knots on Border/ Gold....680
Bee Lines/ Black....310